Professional Persuasion

Wes Lee

Published by Wes Lee, 2020.

While every precaution has been taken in the preparation of this book, the publisher assumes no responsibility for errors or omissions, or for damages resulting from the use of the information contained herein.

PROFESSIONAL PERSUASION

First edition. September 7, 2020.

Written by Wes Lee.

Also by Wes Lee

Impactful Leadership

You Have A Purpose

You Are Rich

You Are Successful

You Are Free

The Brave Bunch (Children's Book)

Watch for more at

I dedicate this book to you. Your commitment to sales and marketing inspires me.

Introduction

Welcome to Professional Persuasion: A 10 Step process, to increase your sales and influence your clients with integrity. Congratulations on stepping up and making the decision to take your life to level 10. I'm so proud of you for committing to improve yourself. The average person talks about growing themselves, but very few do. So, for taking action, I commend you on a wise decision. I've had a distinct honor of working alongside some of the most brilliant CEOs and top influencers, as well as regular work from home moms and dads with an above-average hunger to succeed. Among all of these fantastic people, I noticed one truth that was always consistent; the most significant skill we have is our ability to persuade others. Persuasion and influence come down to our level of connection with ourselves; they affect everything about us, and others. Therefore, they affect how we raise our children; they affect our finances, our careers, and how we treat our health. The people who master persuasion, master the ability to motivate themselves, move other people's emotions, and have an incredible impact on what other people do. The professional

persuader is a true leader who gives far

more than himself or herself. This 10-day

process will help you become an expert

persuader in each area of your life.

Mastering the ability to influence, is about

learning principles to increase your sales.

This book helps you improve your quality of

life, create more possibilities, and bring to

light new distinctions that will serve you. It's

your choice, how you'd like to attack this

book, if you're looking to make the most of

your results, I have three recommendations

for you:

1.   **Interact:** When asked a question, respond to it out loud with enthusiasm, as if we were sitting in the same room.

2.   **Use the book** to review strategies, concepts, and complete assignments.

3.   **Keep your notes with you:** Use them before presentations, prospecting calls, and any crucial interactions. Everything is affected by your Persuasion abilities. I sincerely wish for you to enjoy this book, and I thank you for allowing me to serve you as you transform

your life and the lives of those

around you. Keep in mind all of your

accomplishments up to this point,

and everything you still dream of

accomplishing-come from your

ability to help other people get what

they want. Let's Get Started!

Decision Day

No matter If you're a salesperson, parent, or person who wants to connect with other people, persuasion is one of the most important abilities to master. We need to be able to influence every day, not only other people, but our communities, and ourselves as well. Your persuasion ability is a reflection on your ability to raise a family, advance your career, live a healthy lifestyle, and build meaningful friendships. Becoming a professional persuader and influencer is an essential skill to master in life. It gives you the power to shape your destiny, alter your quality of life, and help those you care about the most. Who are some of the greatest persuaders of our time? Nelson Mandela, Mother Theresa, Gandhi? They persuaded others and powerfully influenced people's thinking to make a tremendous difference in this world. If you seek, you shall find, if you search for people's deepest needs, (instead of what they say they *want)* If you search for their instinctual wants and help them meet them, your income, friendships, and joy will have no limits. It's decision time! If you decide right now, to master becoming a professional persuader, to help influence people to create a better life. If you choose to cut yourself off from any other possibility than mastering this material, you will succeed!

Four Steps to Learning: How do we go from being new to mastering anything? Abraham Maslow, a Humanistic Psychologist, described four steps to learning:

- **Unconscious Incompetence**: You don't know what you don't know

(You have no idea that you don't know how to ride a bike).

- **Conscious Incompetence**: You're aware that you don't know something. (Awareness that you don't know how to ride a bike)

- **Conscious Competence**: You learn something, and it takes your entire concentration. (You learn to ride a bike, and it takes all your focus to balance and not fall)

- **Unconscious Competence**: You've mastered it. You can do something without thinking about it. (You can ride a bike, without focusing on balance or focusing on riding, It becomes automatic)

Five-Step Mastery Process

1.   **Change** - To change anything in your life, and make things how you want them, you must create an impact on yourself.

2.   **Repetition** – Doing something over and over again makes you a master.

3.   **Execution** – Taking action and repeating it in your everyday life.

4.   **Habits** – When you turn these skills into daily habits, they become automatic and effortless.

5.   **Utilization** – To stay sharp, continue utilizing your new skill. Otherwise, you'll lose it.

Success Secrets From The World's Best

The best in the world give 100%

every day! They have crystal clear reasons

for tapping their full abilities.

Discover your "WHY" and the

"HOW" becomes effortless.

---

10 Top Strategies Of The

Best Sellers

1. Ability to change their emotions

instantly

2. Manage their clients' emotions

3. Prepare themselves physically and

emotionally

4. Build high levels of trust

5. Create interest and sustain it

6. Effectively prospect and enjoy it

7. Find clients deepest needs

8. Give clients ways to justify a

purchase

9. Close sales and gain commitments

10. Create an ongoing relationship after

the sale and create sales leverage.

["Success is nothing more than a

few simple disciplines practiced

every day"] - Jim Rohn –

Your Decision To Master

Persuasion

If you've decided you're going to master becoming a professional persuader and influencer, I'd like for you to make some promises to yourself now.

1.   I promise I will push myself.

I promise to take this step because:

2.   I promise I will maintain a high level of energy.

I promise to take this step because:

3. **I promise to be flexible.**

    I promise to take this step because:

4. **I promise to be 100% responsible**

for what I get out of this book

    I promise to take this step because:

Signed:

_____

_____

What's the big difference between the top persuaders and the mediocre ones? They're crystal clear on WHY they must get themselves to finish. Give yourself compelling reasons to excel and become a professional persuader. Reflect on the following questions and answer them.

What's your WHY for mastering this material right now?

How will it positively affect the quality of life for you and those you love?

Why is becoming a professional persuader a

"must" for you?

["People don't buy for logical

reasons, they buy for emotional

reasons."] – Zig Ziglar –

Persuasion Science: Why People Buy

People need to feel some sort of motivation towards buying your products or services. They won't purchase unless they feel the pressure. Pressure comes in two different forms:

- **Outside influence** forms externally from a salesperson or a T.V. ad, for example.

- **Self-pressure** comes from inside a person when they have a desire for something.

Between the two, which do you believe is more powerful? *Self-pressure* is much more potent because people always purchase for their reasons.

Pleasure And Pain

People do things that give them enjoyment and avoid situations that make them feel a sense of pain. People are far more motivated to avoid a painful feeling than to gain a feeling of pleasure. If someone doesn't make a purchase, it means they associate more pain with the buying than emotions of joy, from having your products or services. Conversely, if someone buys from you, they associate more feelings of happiness with their purchase than not making the purchase. As a professional persuader, we must drive our clients by consequences. Negative consequences if they don't buy from you, and positive outcomes if they do.

What The Prospect Is

Thinking

- Will your products or services satisfy my wants and needs?

- What's in this for me? Can you prove it to me? What is it?

- Why do I need your product or service now?

- Can you be trusted? Am I a transaction, or are you here to serve my interests?

The Persuasion Process

The process of Influencing and persuading another person is about finding people's pain points, opening the pain tactfully, and then healing their pain points by providing them new solutions in your products or services.

1.   Find their deepest wants: People won't buy something they don't feel they need. They purchase what they want.

2. **Find their pain points:** Your job is to use your products or services to heal them.

3. **Show them how to heal their pain points:** By getting your clients to associate their most desired feelings to your products or services.

["Everything you and I do, we do either out of our need to avoid pain or our desire to gain pleasure"] Tony Robbins

A Client That Isn't

Motivated Won't

Purchase

Professional persuaders are masters
of helping clients associate their products or
services with the client's feelings of desire.
Professional persuaders also get the clients
to link not purchasing with the client's
deepest pain points.

- People have **EMOTIONAL**
  reasons they buy.

- People have **LOGICAL** reasons they buy.

- People have **MAJOR** reasons they don't buy.

Professional Influencing And Persuading

We want a person's emotional and logical reasons to overwhelm the significant reasons they don't buy. It's tough to close without a lot of anxiety or excitement for your products or services.

1.   If the sale is on the fence,

bring up their pain points, which will

create more WANT.

2.   Add emotional reasons they

need to buy.

3.   Then add logical reasons to

help them justify the purchase

(you'll need a lot of desire or pain).

Activity

1.   List out three things you desired but didn't end up buying. Why didn't you? And how many emotional, logical, and significant reasons did you have for not purchasing?

2.   Choose an item you didn't buy. What would have kicked you over the edge and closed the sale?

3.   Choose three items you desired and ended up purchasing. Why did you buy it? How much

emotion was behind your decision?

What was your logic for buying?

What primary reasons came to mind

for not purchasing?

Remember: People buy on emotion and

justify logically

How To Create Massive

Influence

1.   **Questions:** Your most important tool in persuading another person is to ask them questions. Questions build considerable rapport; you discover the person's beliefs, and how they make decisions. You show them how your products or services align with what they already believe. Questions help you:

- Put people into an excellent emotional framework
- Build massive rapport
- Alleviate pressure

- Discover beliefs

- Find out how a person thinks

- Bring out objections upfront

- Build a relationship on

  reciprocity

- Demonstrate care

- Test close or temperature check

- Discover what motivates the

  person

2.   **Emotional Discipline:** It's

necessary to have control over your

emotions, especially if someone

cancels appointments, and doesn't

keep their word. Lack of discipline reduces your ability to influence and persuade effectively. When you effectively discipline your emotions, you can take negative situations, like broken commitments, and turn them into positives that will empower you.

3.   **Rapport:** To build long-term relationships, people must feel that you care about them, you put them first, and that you are both alike. When you're in alignment with people, you've built rapport, and you

can lead them in the direction you'd

like.

How To Create Rapport:

- Listen

- Make a comment that shocks them

- Give Free Samples

- Give referrals

- Discover mutual interests

- Give outstanding service

- Give a genuine compliment

- Tell stories

- Give a gift

1. **Congruency** means what you say and who you are is a match. You're in alignment and feel sure about what you say—feeling confident that the value of your product or service far exceeds the cost. Buying means transferring emotions; it's your self-assurance that will help people feel confident when they buy. Refresh this discipline daily because we can fall victim to the Law of Familiarity, taking our products or services for granted.

Persuasion Science Final Assignment

Look over the ways to create massive influence. Identify the one you're weakest with and complete this assignment with that in mind.

1.   **Questions:** Write 3 to 5 questions that will engage people:

2.   **Emotional Discipline:** Describe in detail how you need to feel when you are persuading and

influencing. How would your body look? What will you be saying?

3.   **Rapport:** Make a promise to yourself that you will build rapport with at least three people within the next 24 hours. List HOW you will accomplish this.

4.   **Congruency:** Create an empowering short story to tell yourself over and over again. Practice telling yourself that story, in the mirror, with belief and emotion.

["You must be the change you wish to see in the world"] – Mahatma Gandhi -

Belief

Our beliefs are the difference
between our success and failure. Your
actions are determined by what you
believe. How much would your level of
effort increase, if you truly understand that
what you're doing will bring you more joy,
and financial abundance? Lots of people set
goals or set resolutions, but this isn't
enough. You must believe you can achieve
your goals.

["No one can defeat us unless we first defeat ourselves"] – Dwight Eisenhower –

Types Of Beliefs

1.   Blanket Beliefs:

-   "You are…"

-   "I am…"

-   "The world is…"

-   "The rich are…"

These Blanket beliefs color what things mean to you and how you view them. Professional persuaders use questions to discover the clients' expectations and align with them. Never attack a person's belief system.

2.   **Cause and Effect Beliefs:**

- "If I do **X**... then it is going to mean **Y**." These beliefs help to give your decisions a guiding light.

Activity

When you're persuading, you're transferring your emotions and feelings to your clients. You can't transfer feelings that you don't have! Selling means overcoming questions. Before you face an objection (an issue), you need to believe that whatever happens, you can handle it.

Refer back to the questions clients always ask themselves before making a purchase.

This exercise helps you think about the client's needs, guide them with integrity, and build your belief.

- Why is your product or service worth far more than its cost, in terms of time, money, and value-added to the client?

- Why do you care about your clients? How do they know you won't take advantage of them? What is your belief system about this?

- How will your clients be able to justify (logically) this purchase to others? How will the people around the client also benefit?

- What are the benefits your client will enjoy, what will this mean to other people, and what are your interests?

- Why should your clients purchase your products or services?

Why People Don't Reach Their Potential

- **They don't have strong enough reasons** for success when it inevitably becomes challenging.

- **They don't discipline their emotions** because the ability to temper our feelings is the difference between success and failure.

- **Their beliefs are limited.** Maybe they've tried in the past, and nothing seemed to work, or they

can't see how something could

work, and they've already future

projected -what they believe will

happen.

["Don't be pushed around by the

fears in your mind. Be led by the

dreams in your heart"] – Roy T.

Bennett

The Importance Of

Emotional Discipline

Our *thoughts* control our *feelings,*
which control our *actions,* which control our
results. Your performance is directly related
to the way you feel and your mood or state.
You're not ultimately selling your products
or services; you're selling your emotions. If
you have a great attitude, and you speak
with your client about your product, they
will relate your positive emotions to your
products or services. It works the same if

you're in a negative place. So the question is, how do you change the way you're feeling, and bring yourself into that positive place, anytime, anywhere?

Changing Your Emotional State

Change how you're using your body

- Move a different way.

- Change your diet, and when you eat.

- Change your breathing pattern.

- Create actions that raise your emotions. For example, my team and I use to stand up, get in a circle, clap, and to chant our motto. We engaged and tapped into our best emotions before work.

Become more aware of your focus

- How you feel is determined by your mind at any moment.
- Ask yourself better questions, to control your focus. What are some powerful questions you could ask yourself? What could

you ask yourself to elevate your

feelings right before meeting

with a client?

Develop Daily Habits

- Ask yourself powerfully positive

  questions.

- Move your body differently, like

  clapping, snapping your fingers,

  and getting yourself pumped.

- Make 12-15 Swish Patterns

Swish Patterns

I learned these patterns from Tony

Robbins:

What negative image keeps you from reaching success? Craft a picture of the person you'd be if you accomplished your goals. Bring your positive image behind your negative image in your mind and make it larger until it bursts through the negative image. As you do this, reach your right hand out, say SWISH, and drive your right arm back in like a fist pump. Do this until your negative image is hard to recall.

Belief Final Assignment

1.   Write out a few more compelling questions that will raise your emotional level.

2.   As soon as you wake up tomorrow, stand up and do the action you created to put you in a top emotional state. Get in motion, whether it's clapping, snapping your fingers, pushups, swinging your arms, whatever it is.

3.   Tomorrow morning after you get into action, ask yourself some new questions:

- What can I be grateful for at this moment?

- What excites me today?

- What makes me happy about this new day?

["Yesterday is not ours to recover,

but tomorrow is ours to win or lose"

] – Lyndon B. Johnson

The Sales Phases

The most successful persuaders and influencers always execute a sale, in the same way, using the same order of steps.

1. **Involvement –** Interacting with clients, getting them involved, grabbing their attention, contacting them, and creating interest.

2. **Qualify and Magnify –** Discover their deepest pain points, and qualify them. Making sure they

feel good about your product or

service and that they want to

purchase.

3.   **Urgency** – Elicit an emotional

state where they want to buy right

now. Ensuring we close after

qualifying them and magnifying their

pain points. We're signing them up.

The Sales Phase Steps

Phase 1: Involvement

1. **Preparation**

2. **Your Peak Emotional State**

3. **Contact Your Clients**

4. **Build a Deep Relationship**

5. **Captivate Them**

Phase 2: Qualify And Magnify

6. **Qualify Clients and Magnify Pain Points**

7. **Cultivate Their Belief and Test Close**

Phase 3: Urgency

8. **Make it Tangible and Take an Assumptive Posture**

Involvement (Phase 1)

Sales Step 1: Preparation

When we feel nervous and reluctant to engage our clients, it stems from a lack of preparation. Don't fall into the trap. Know your clients, your products, and be prepared to make the sales.

How To Prepare:

- **Know Your Clients and Anticipate Their Needs, Wants, and Pain Points:** Research as much as you can about your client's needs and wants. How do they spend their money and time? Use sources like the internet, referrals, friends, and co-workers.

- **Understand your Competitors:** Know the advantages your products or services have. Be tactful, and never speak badly about competitors

- **Create desire:** by creating situations where clients convince themselves of the value of your offer, for their reasons.

- **Have a Positive Expectation:** Be ready for the worst, but expect the best. Place yourself in a positive emotional frame while being prepared for changes.

- **Have a Deep Understanding of your Products or Services:** Create a list of the benefits that matter to your clients. This list should be so detailed you'll have an abundance of reasons your

clients must buy.

- **Prepare in advance for the Most**

  Common Objections: Be ready

  to know precisely how to handle

  these before they come up.

Sales Step 2: Your Peak

Emotional State

Being at your peak emotional frame
means you consciously put yourself in place
to produce exceptional results.

Your peak performance comes from your

peak emotional state.

Change Your Body

The fastest way to change the way you feel is to change how you're using your physiology.

1.   Pick an empowering word. I prefer **YES!** And a physical motion, as we discussed earlier (clapping, jumping, snapping your fingers).

2.   Link your emotions to that word (think of an anchor).

3.   You change your body by getting in motion and using an empowering word.

Using an internal 1-10 scale, what

level is your emotional frame? Your goal is

to feel far beyond a ten before engaging

your clients.

["Disease cannot live in a body

that's in a healthy emotional state"

] – Bob Proctor –

Sales Step 2: Selling Is About Transferring Emotions

Whenever you're in front of your clients, your feelings affect your clients. Interacting with your clients out of your peak emotional frame diminishes your abilities and skills to persuade.

- **People directly associate your feelings and emotions to your**

products or services: If you're in a negative place, your negativity affects what you're selling.

- **You also associate your own emotions to your products or services:** If you feel bad, you'll talk about your product with those same bad feelings.

Emotions affect every relationship you have. Any time you're in a powerful emotional state (positive or negative), those emotions become attached to anything happening around you. In the future, that same situation will trigger those same

emotions in you.

Activity

1.   How will your life transform in the next five years, if you consistently discipline your emotional frame? How will your career look? What kind of additional money will you make? How much more will you enjoy your life?

2.   Describe your life, as you see it, in the next five years if you decide not to change? What will the price be?

3.   How much have you already lost in the past few years, by not disciplining your emotions? Add up your missed opportunities because you didn't feel like it, weren't prepared, or you didn't follow through.

4.   What has your emotional price been in the last few years? How much has not disciplining your emotions cost in terms of frustration, regret, anger, and resentment?

Sales Step 3: Contact Your

Clients

Once you're prepared, and in the

right emotional frame, nothing will move

until you contact your clients and draw their

attention to you.

The Law of Averages goes to work here.

The more contacts you make, the more

money you make.

Making Great Connections

- **Have a plan for what you'll say:**
  Use a Script and know your focus
  with the client. Practice, so
  you're not focused on what to
  say next.

- **Make a ton of contacts:** Call and
  set appointments with as many
  people as you can, at your peak
  emotional state.

- **Get creative and have fun:** Find
  new and innovative ways to
  make contact with your clients.

When you make it fun, you make
it enjoyable for yourself as well.

- **Set goals that are specific and
  measurable:** Decide on the
  number of contacts you'll make
  on a weekly, monthly, and yearly
  basis.

- **Always ask for referrals:**
  Whether the client purchases or
  not, ask for references. Set up
  your next sale, before your
  current deal is over.

Reasons People Don't

Make Contact:

- They're unprepared

- They're not in their peak

  emotional frame

- They believe they will be

  interrupting

You're only interrupting a client until you

have the client's attention.

How Do We Get The Clients' Attention?

- **Compliment –** What do you genuinely like about your client? Tell them with feeling.

- **Demonstration –** Show the client something or exhibit your product or service.

- **Intrigue –** Ask an engaging question or create some suspense.

- **Additional Information –** Offer additional information that your client is interested in, and doesn't have already.
- **Pain Points –** Stir up some emotion, regarding their hurts, to get their full attention.
- **Smile –** Already being in a positive state when you meet your client.
- **Referrals –** Utilize a reference to build instant rapport through third-party validation.
- **Questions –** Ask a question that grabs attention.

Keep In Mind:

You're selling your emotional state

and transferring feelings to clients.

Step 3 Final Assignment

Professional persuaders ALWAYS

implement the strategies for making great

connections:

- **Have a plan for what you'll say.**

- **Make a ton of contacts**

- **Get creative and have fun**

- **Set goals that are specific and**

  measurable

- **Always ask for referrals**

As soon as you're impressive enough to capture the clients' attention, they'll make time for you. Make contacts, get the clients' attention, engage, and have fun with the process!

["A dream becomes a goal when action is taken towards its achievement"] – Bo Bennett –

Sales Step 4: Build A Deep Relationship

Recap:

So far, you've learned about the three initial phases of being a professional persuader.

1. **Involvement**
2. **Qualify and Magnify**
3. **Urgency**

In the first phase, you learned the three

initial steps:

1.   **Preparation**

2.   **Your Peak Emotional State**

3.   **Contact Your Clients**

When two people meet, some things begin to happen, that generate trust, friendships, rapport, and confidence. When you understand the factors, you're able to create rapport and connect with people, consistently. You can do this in a way that feels warm and sincere. So why will a client choose your products and services over someone else with the same offering? Client's will choose you because they trust you, they like you, and they have confidence in your ability to deliver what you said you would. When they want you, they believe over others, that you have their best interests at heart, and that you will always put them first. In this section, you'll learn how to create these feelings within your clients.

Professional persuaders understand that the essential part of any sale isn't the closing process. It's building rapport with their clients. When you want to persuade and influence someone strongly, the most critical quality is *trust*. The client needs to have faith in you if you wish to change and help them long-term. The old saying "People don't care how much you know until they know how much you care" rings so true! People buy from people they're close to, people they like.

The Power Of

Compliments

Compliments are one of the best ways to connect with someone quickly. There's a right way and a wrong way to give praise. Effective praise will make a person feel validated, appreciated, and served. An ineffective compliment will come off as flattery. I'll show you how to deliver compliments the right way:

1.   Tell the person something that you sincerely like or appreciate about the person.

2. Use the word "Because" to justify your delivering of the compliment

3. End the compliment by asking the person a question related to the praise.

It's the power of asking a sincere question, that makes your compliment more genuine. You're demonstrating care and curiosity for your client.

How To Use Compliments

- Deliver compliments about other people; they will get back to the subject of the praise.

- Provide a tribute that shows you are paying attention to small details about the client.

- Write a thank-you note to your clients.

- Deliver 3rd party compliments, and let the client know what other people like about them.

Activity

Choose three people in your life and write out a compliment for each, using the criteria above. Promise yourself that you will give each of those people, your genuine praise, within the next 24 hours.

1.

2.

3.

["The Real Gift of Gratitude is the more grateful you are, the more present you become"] - Robert Holden –

Developing Massive

Rapport

1. **Mirroring -** A compelling way to connect with your clients is to reflect their actions. Everything from their rate of speech, the way they

speak, their body language, and the words they use. The most important is to match their body language, which makes up more than half of all communication.

2.   Search for commonalities - People like people who are like each other. People tend to dislike people who aren't like them. The more you have in common, the more you'll like each other. The less you have in common, the less rapport you'll build.

Using our voices and body language

to match others, we can create

rapport with anyone.

Qualities To Mirror And Copy

Voice - Keywords, volume, vocal tonality, tempo, timbre.

Body language - Movements, facial expressions, gestures, eye contact, breathing patterns, physical proximity, kinesthetics (touching), body posture.

3.   **Go at The client's speed -** Match yourself at the same pace as

your client for a little bit. Then begin
to change the pace of the
interaction, and you'll notice the
client will unconsciously follow your
pace.

Different Styles Of

Communication

We process information with our
five senses: sight, touch, smell, sight, and
hearing. The three most common are sight,
touch, and auditory. We also process

information through the 4th style of communication called: digital. Digital relies on pure logic and details. Most people you'll meet have developed one communication style they prefer to use more frequently. We, as professional persuaders, need to know and understand a client's communication preference.

Feel - People who prefer to communicate through feeling, speak, and consider things more slowly and quietly.

Visual - Speak louder, and faster, they have pictures running through their heads, they tend to move more quickly, and say things like "Take a look at this" or "Imagine that"

Digital - Make decisions through logic primarily. Facts and data are most important to the digital communicator.

Hearing - Tend to articulate their words more, and are more selective about what they say. Their movements tend to have a rhythm.

To effectively deliver information to each communication style, we must understand them so that we can enter the client's world.

Step 4 Final Assignment

Choose a person to mirror in conversation. Pay attention to the effects you have. How did the tone of the discussion change? Did the person respond positively? How quickly did you establish rapport? Are you able to start the interaction at their pace and then change it to yours?

Record What You've

Observed:

["Your mind is your greatest power, use it well"] - Aneta Cruz –

Sales Step 5: Captivate Them

Most people in sales go right into the presentation when the client isn't yet interested in hearing what they have to say. It's a total waste of time if you don't have genuine interest from your clients! In this step, your goal is to get your client excited to hear more. If you don't captivate their attention, they won't truly listen to what you have to say.

The Word "Because."

As people, we tend to justify what we do. The word "because" is compelling, even if what you say after doesn't make any sense. Often, most people will go along with you anyways, if your reasons for doing something are justified.

How To Captivate Your Clients

- **Talk about something they know or someone they know** to provide your clients with Social Proof.

- **Ask Questions** Because:

1. When you show interest in someone, they will, in turn, show interest in you.

2. It allows your clients to be in control.

3. You focus the clients' attention on what they want and create even more interest.

- **Demonstrate** Show your product or service and find ways to make your clients part of the experience.

Captivate Them With Benefits

1. **Claim something about your product or service** that interests your client.

2.   Follow-up with a logical fact that begins with the word "Because" to justify it.

3.   Tell the client how it will benefit them. Clients want to know, "What's in it for me!"

4.   Follow-up with another more emotional benefit. What will having your products or services do for them emotionally? What does it mean to this client?

5.   Give the client evidence of your claim. You want to provide something concrete to support your statements.

6.   Ask an open-ended question about their wants and needs

["A Dream doesn't become a reality through magic; it takes sweat, determination, and hard work"] - Colin Powell –

Gaining Trust And Belief In Your Products Or Services

- Deliver a testimonial. You can keep letters with you or save emails.

- Showcase your product or service to display the quality of what you have.

- Provide evidence through stories and examples. These can be from your team members.

- Show the client data that can be verified.

- Relate your product or service to something the client understands with analogies.

- Provide facts about your products, services, or your business.

- Demonstrate what you're selling. When it works the way you claim, there won't be disbelief.

Step 5 Final Assignment

Craft a reason for your product or

service, that will captivate your client, using

the six steps from earlier.

1.   **Claim Something about your**

Products or Service

2.   **Follow-up with a logical fact**

3.   Tell the client how it will

benefit them

4.   Follow-up with another

more emotional benefit

5.   Give the client evidence of

your claim

6.   Ask an open-ended question

about their wants and needs

["Persistent People begin their

Success where others fail"] -

Edward Eggleston –

Qualify And Magnify

(Phase 2)

Way to go! You finished the first

phase of becoming a professional

persuader. So far, you've learned how to:

1.   **Prepare**

2.   Unleash Your Peak

Emotional State

3.   Contact Your Clients

4.   Build Deep Relationships

5.   Captivate Your Clients

Now let's move on to Phase 2:

Qualify and Magnify:

6. Qualify Clients and Magnify Pain

Points

7. Cultivate their Belief and Test

Close

Think of a time when you were with a client and went through a full presentation just to find out they couldn't make the purchase, or your product wasn't right for their needs. We face these challenges in business and our personal life. Maybe there was a time when you blamed a family member for something they didn't do. Perhaps you planned to talk your significant other out of a purchase, that they never intended to make in the first place. In all these examples, the person wasn't adequately qualified first! Qualifying is an integral part of any sale.

Sales Step 6: Qualify Clients And Magnify Pain Points

Persuading is hugely lucrative and fulfilling, as long as your intention as a professional persuader is to find people's pains and heal them. If you see yourself as a leader with a service mindset, you'll feel a deep sense of accomplishment, and you'll get paid very well. As Zig Ziglar said: "We can have anything we want in life, as long as we help enough people get what they want." Average salespeople don't know and understand their clients. They don't know what clients need, who they are, or how they make their buying decisions. Average salespeople try to find out a little about the client, do a full presentation, and hard close. This step will teach you what clients need, what they want, how they make decisions, and how they justify their purchases.

Qualifying Your Clients

Our goal is to get people to associate their pains with not having something. When we qualify prospects, we need to know their deepest needs and problems. Where is your client unfulfilled? Discover their pain points and magnify them; you'll create a desire for your solution. Creating a deep passion for your product or service gives the client plenty of emotional reasons (benefits) to purchase from you. They also have plenty of reasons to feel hurt if they don't buy it.

Questions For Qualifying Prospects

- **Wants -** What does your client honestly WANT?

- **Pain -** What are your client's pain points?

- **Needs -** What does your client need?

- **Income -** Does your client have the money?

- **Decision -** Can your client make the final decision on purchasing?

Do they have the authority? Or do they have to decide with someone else?

It's an absolute must that you qualify the client with these five criteria before you waste valuable time. Don't go through a full presentation, just to find out they don't have the want, pain point, need, money, or decision-making power to purchase from you.

Activity

Write out three to five questions that you can ask your clients to discover who they are. Then, qualify them.

Wants:

1.

2.

3.

4.

5.

Pain:

1.

2.

3.

4.

5.

Needs:

1.

2.

3.

4.

5.

Income:

1.

2.

3.

4.

5.

Decision:

1.

2.

3.

4.

5.

People's Patterns Of

Thought

People all have patterns for coloring

their world. Knowing people's patterns of

thoughts can help you deliver information in

a way that will help them make the best

decision. These are ways you can identify their trends:

1.   A frame of Reference (Internally or Externally Motivated)

Question: How do you know when you've done an outstanding job? Do you feel it inside, or do you need someone to acknowledge your work?

People who are internally motivated prefer making decisions by looking within themselves. People who are externally motivated look to other people to acknowledge and validate that they've done an excellent job. To captivate internal people, find out what they value and describe your product or service with that in mind. To captivate external people, use things like statistics, data, and testimonials to show them what other people think.

2.   **Patterns of motivation**

3.   ***Observe* the client's actions:** Clients are interested in how their purchase will affect other people, themselves, or the numbers.

4.   **What's possible or what's needed:** *Question:* What made you choose your current career or product?

Some clients will be inspired by what could be possible in the future. Others are inspired only when they feel like your products or services are something they need. To motivate people who focus on what's possible, paint a picture of the future, and what could happen. To encourage people who focus on what's required, show them what they need to do.

5. **Polarity:** Clients who are of positive polarity seek out how things are alike. Clients of an opposite polarity always focus on the differences. Positive polarity people either see everything as the same, or they understand that almost everything is the same with some differences. To inspire and motivate a person who sees everything the same, compare your products or services to something positive they've experienced in their past. People with opposite polarity personalities do the opposite of everything you say. Or, every time

you present possibilities, they offer

you an example that goes against

what you said. To inspire and

motivate Opposite polarity people

who do everything the opposite of

you, use reverse psychology and

encourage them to do the opposite

of what you want them to do. To

inspire people who have examples

for everything opposite to your

standards, present them with cases

that are opposite of what you

believe before they have the chance

to give you their examples.

6.   **Push or Pull:** *Question:* What are your WANTS in a career or a product? "Pull" clients become inspired and motivated by gaining pleasure and desiring. They're "pulled" towards it. "push" clients become encouraged to act based on fear and pain points (when they feel "pushed" away). To inspire a "pull" client to take action, paint a picture of goals to achieve and rewards they can receive. To encourage a "push" client to act, describe the consequences of not purchasing and speak about their pain points.

7. Value vs. Price Tag:

Question: What means more to you: The quality of the product/service or how cost-effective it is? As Americans, we tend to value things that make our life more comfortable, and we are often willing to pay a little more for that convenience. Other parts of the world value cost over perceived quality.

8.   Finisher vs. Process-Oriented: *Question:* What gives you more fulfillment, finishing something, or your involvement in the process? Clients who are finishers quite literally must finish what they start. Clients who are more process-oriented enjoy the journey. They may want to meet with you several times before closing a sale.

9.   The Forest vs. The Trees: *Question:* What do you value more: The overview of something or the details? People who are like the forest want the grand picture, the summary, and care less about the granular details. Clients who are like the trees value the details. Don't provide "the forest" client a bunch of small details, and don't try to give "The trees" client the big picture view.

10. **Past vs. Future:** *Question: What do you value more: How a product/service did in it's past or the possibilities of how it will do in the future?* A past focused client wants to see that your product or service HAS HAD longevity and has a track record. A future-focused client wants to know where your product/service is going and the possibilities ahead.

11.   **Belief:** *Question:* When do you believe someone is good at what they do? Are you convinced when you see it, read it, do it with them, or hear about it? What kind of evidence does the client require to believe you? Sight, hearing, feeling, or data? What is the

timeframe it takes for your client to

trust you? Does it happen

automatically, is it a few exposures,

a significant time after, or do they

always need to be re-reminded to

believe?

Step 6 Final Assignment

Speak with the people around you
and see how many of these patterns of
thought you're able to figure out. Write
your observations.

Sales Step 7: Cultivate Their Belief And Test Close

After you've done a great job with the first six initial steps, here's where you'll be at:

1. You know the client: You understand their needs and pain points. You have a strong understanding of who you compete with, and your products/services and you've created a game plan.

2. You're in a peak emotional state:

To deliver your information

powerfully.

3. You've reached out to your

clients

4. You've connected: You've built

trust, and your client knows they're

working with a professional.

5. You've intrigued your clients:

Clients feel like you've put them

first. They also understand what you

have, how it will benefit them and

have seen the proof, backing up

what you say.

6. The client is qualified: You now know their wants, needs, pain points, if they can make the final purchasing decision, and whether they have the income.

Next, you'll give your clients reasons to help them justify (logically) why they should buy. And, you'll do a temperature check (test close) to see where they're at in the sales process.

Sales Step 7: Cultivate Belief And Test Close

We want to cultivate the belief that you can meet the person's needs.

Creating Belief And Justification

- **Create enough compelling reasons:** Both emotionally and logically, that the client should purchase from you. Remember, these emotional and logical reasons have to overpower their ideas for not making a purchase. Plenty of these reasons will overwhelm any reason not to purchase from you.

- **What you say on the outside matches your feelings inside.** You need a deep belief in your product. You and the client have to believe with certainty that buying your products/services will fulfill their deepest desires.

- Give clients enough compelling reasons to justify their purchase logically.

1. Claim something about your products or services

2. Follow up with a logical fact

3. Tell the client how it will benefit them

4. Follow-up with another more emotional benefit

5. Give the client evidence of your claim

6. Ask open-ended questions about their wants and needs

With an Important added step

7.   **Test close**: Start with a powerful phrase ("I'd like your opinion... How do you feel...")

A Test Close Vs. A Close

When you're doing a test close, you're asking the opinion of a client. You're also creating a *hypothetical* and finding out "what" they would do "if" something happened. Test closing is the best for getting the objections out. Test closing will

empower you to know *when* to close.

Activity

Write out a dozen convincing reasons to create belief and trust in your clients. Practice these and put them in your toolbox when you need compelling reasons that clients should purchase from you.

First Reason:

1. Claim something about your products or services

2. Follow up with a logical fact

3. Tell the client how it will benefit them

4. Follow-up with another more emotional benefit

5. Give the client evidence of your claim

6. Ask open-ended questions about their wants and needs

Second Reason:

1. Claim something about your products or services

2. Follow up with a logical fact

3. Tell the client how it will benefit them

4. Follow-up with another more emotional benefit

5. Give the client evidence of your claim

6. Ask open-ended questions about their wants and needs

Third Reason:

1. Claim something about your products or services

2. Follow up with a logical fact

3. Tell the client how it will benefit them

4. Follow-up with another more emotional benefit

5. Give the client evidence of your claim

6. Ask open-ended questions about their wants and needs

Fourth Reason:

1. Claim something about your products or services

2. Follow up with a logical fact

3. Tell the client how it will benefit them

4. Follow-up with another more emotional benefit

5. Give the client evidence of your claim

6. Ask open-ended questions about their wants and needs

Fifth Reason:

1. Claim something about your products or services

2. Follow up with a logical fact

3. Tell the client how it will benefit them

4. Follow-up with another more emotional benefit

5. Give the client evidence of your claim

6. Ask open-ended questions about their wants and needs

Sixth Reason:

1. Claim something about your products or services

2. Follow up with a logical fact

3. Tell the client how it will benefit them

4. Follow-up with another more emotional benefit

5. Give the client evidence of your claim

6. Ask open-ended questions about their wants and needs

Seventh Reason

1. Claim something about your products or services

2. Follow up with a logical fact

3. Tell the client how it will benefit them

4. Follow-up with another more emotional benefit

5. Give the client evidence of your claim

6. Ask open-ended questions about their wants and needs

Eighth Reason:

1. Claim something about your products or services

2. Follow up with a logical fact

3. Tell the client how it will benefit them

4. Follow-up with another more emotional benefit

5. Give the client evidence of your claim

6. Ask open-ended questions about their wants and needs

Ninth Reason:

1. Claim something about your products or services

2. Follow up with a logical fact

3. Tell the client how it will benefit them

4. Follow-up with another more emotional benefit

5. Give the client evidence of your claim

6. Ask open-ended questions about their wants and needs

Tenth Reason:

1. Claim something about your products or services

2. Follow up with a logical fact

3. Tell the client how it will benefit them

4. Follow-up with another more emotional benefit

5. Give the client evidence of your claim

6. Ask open-ended questions about their wants and needs

Eleventh Reason:

1. Claim something about your products or services

2. Follow up with a logical fact

3. Tell the client how it will benefit them

4. Follow-up with another more emotional benefit

5. Give the client evidence of your claim

6. Ask open-ended questions about their wants and needs

Twelfth Reason:

1. Claim something about your products or services

2. Follow up with a logical fact

3. Tell the client how it will benefit them

4. Follow-up with another more emotional benefit

5. Give the client evidence of your claim

6. Ask open-ended questions about their wants and needs

Internalize each of these, so you're able to deliver them when you need a reason to push your clients over

the edge, help them purchase, and

justify their decision.

Ways to Test Close

1. Opening Test Close

Purpose: To find where your client's at in the sales process.

For Example: Why are you seriously considering working from home?

Benefits of this close: This test close will tell you their seriousness and also your client's emotional and logical reasons that they make purchases.

2. Trade-Off Test Close

For Example: Would it be worth **X** to have **Y?** *or* To complete your goal of **X,** would it be worth investing **Y?**

Benefits of this close: You can overwhelm their reasons for not purchasing from you, with the benefits of buying from you.

3. Progressive Test Close

Purpose: To help the client focus on purchasing your product/service.

For Example: If you felt this was a way to take control of your financial future, how would you find a way to make this happen?

The benefit of this close. The client is focusing on the positives, *what they want* instead of *what they don't want*.

These test closes help you see where your client's at; if they're moving *towards* or *away* from purchasing from you. If your client is walking away from buying your products/services, provide more of the convincing reasons you created above.

Test Closing

Your goal is to be doing test closes from the start of your interaction with the client. You don't want to get to the last part of the sale to find out that your client isn't there with you. When you continuously test close your clients, you will notice:

- Where the client is at and what
  actions you'll need to take
- What your potential outcome
  will be
- When to take action and do a
  real close

Client's Buying Physiology

(When To Close)

- **Body Posture:** The client will have a relaxed and comfortable posture.

- **Demeanor:** Your clients will be friendly, and future project your products and services as if they already possess them.

- **Facial Expressions:** Their faces have more color, and they smile more.

- **Hands:** Open palms, clients will also touch their faces and become more kinesthetic with your products/services. They'll want to feel your products and test applications.

Step 7 Final Assignment

Practice each test close by writing out at least three questions for each.

Opening Test Close

Trade-Off Test Close

Progressive Test Close

["If you are not taking care of your

customer, your competitor will"] -

Bob Hooey –

Urgency (Phase 3)

Sales Step 8: Make it Tangible and Take an Assumptive Posture

Look how far we have come since the start of this book! Let's recap:

- You did your preparation
- You placed yourself in a peak emotional state

- You then contacted your client

- When you contacted your client, you captured their attention

- You became close with them, gained a lot of rapport, brought them into the selling process, and engaged their deepest interests.

- Then you dug deeper, found out who they are, what they fear, what inspires them and found your clients' pattern of purchasing.

- You worked with your clients to help them overpower their fears of NOT buying with their emotional and logical reasons that they need to purchase from you.

- In this last phase, we create Urgency and bring this whole sales process to life for your client. Making this tangible is all about getting clients to experience your products or services with all of their senses. We will accomplish this through our final steps:

Step 8: Make it Tangible and take an Assumptive Posture

Step 9: Transform Client Objections Into Client Commitments

Step 10: Create a Lasting Relationship And Make Buying Simple

Making this real for your clients means giving your clients a sensory experience. Experiences have less to do with data and logic, and more to do with showing your clients. Your clients need to see that purchasing from you will bring pleasure; not buying from you will mean continued pain. Make this real, overcome the client's initial objections, and they'll purchase your products/services.

How do you motivate and inspire your clients to purchase your products/services and be persuaded by you? We make their experience real and instill a belief that purchasing your product means fulfillment and pleasure, while not buying means pain. We're tapping into the client's imagination, which is deeper and more potent than their will.

- Clients who purchase believe their buying experience will be more pleasurable.
- Clients who don't buy have linked more pain to the purchase, than pleasure from obtaining it.

When you make their experience tangible, something they can feel with all of their senses, you're in a position to be assumptive that they will buy.

The Power Behind

Questions

Questions induce reciprocity.

Meaning whatever you ask, your client feels

compelled to answer; your questions create

a real experience.

They Also:

- Change the focus of your clients

- You're able to access more

  resources

\-   They change what people keep
and what they remove from their
minds

Giving Your Clients A

Tangible Experience

Professional persuaders are masters
of eliciting emotion in their clients and
giving them an experience that touches all
of their senses. The very best persuaders
and the highest-paid salespeople can bring
out the very best in their clients. By bringing

out the very best in your clients, you'll make

their sales experience even more real.

Direct, Exclaim, Visualize

If clients are still on the fence, we have some strategies to bring them to your side:

Direct: Rephrase what they want back to them.

For example: "You had said you wanted **X** which will provide you **Y.**" Is this still correct?

This Question Should

Direct their mind back to a fear or pain point that they're experiencing. In doing this, you'll create an even greater desire for what you have, by simply reminding your client of what they don't want. Remind them why they're purchasing. *"You had said that you wanted a product that lasts you at least six months with each order. This order will provide you a long-term supply. I remember you had said your product runs out too quickly, and you're tired of overpaying for something that* underperforms. Is this still correct?" "You said that investing in our service would give you peace of mind. With this investment, you'll have a team behind you with the support you need. I remember you said you didn't receive any support in the past, with this service, and you were very frustrated. Is this still correct?" "You shared how important it is to invest in a home that provides your family with the safety and coziness that you always imagined a forever home should have. Is this correct?"

Exclaim: Tell them that your product/service will do, what they are looking to do (If it actually will). Bring up the clients' biggest fear/concern and how your product/service will solve the issue. Then assure your client and make their purchasing experience more tangible. Go into details about what they'll receive from your product/service that will heal their biggest fears and concerns.

Visualize: Paint what life will look like for your clients when they purchase from you. *"When you purchase our services, what will happen is **X**. Is this what you want to have?"* (Describe the place and the time of day in vivid detail) We're tapping into the imagination. *"When you invest in our services, I want you to imagine a Saturday at 8 a.m. during the summer. You expressed that this was your favorite time with your family. Now imagine, you won't get those calls that have been consistently pulling you away from your family every Saturday. Imagine our services having you covered, so you're able to finally enjoy your family and do what is most important to you. Is this what you want to have?"* At this point, we're taking an assumptive posture on the sale.

["Imagination is everything, it is

the preview of Life's Coming

Attractions"] - Albert Einstein –

Step 8 Final Assignment

1. Create at least five compelling

questions that will help your clients

already feel like they own your

products/services. Project into the

future!

- ?

- ?

- ?

- ?

- ?

2. How can you get your clients to feel like they own your products/services already? Step outside the box and create 20 unique and fun things that utilize all of the clients' senses. Create two ideas per day for the next ten days. How can you use all five senses to create an experience that the client associates with what you're selling?

Sales Step 9: Transform Client Objections Into Client Commitments

In my experience, the most significant concern people have is the word "No." People would rather fail, waste time, energy, and money to avoid hearing the word "No." Think about where your mind goes the moment your client objects. Do you get anxious and feel like giving up, or do you feel excited to share a new possibility with them?

- Objections are questions, the client is asking for more information on something that interests them.

- You'll face obstacles before you make a sale. Most salespeople see at least five objections before closing. So, stop for a moment and reflect on this, how do you feel when a client objects to you? How do you currently define objections when they happen? Do you think they are opportunities or challenges? Are they something we should avoid,

or something that should excite

us? In this step, you'll learn how

to take any objection a client

presents and turn it into a

commitment to you. You'll feel

empowered and welcome them

as opportunities.

What Is An Objection?

- Your opportunity to find out

  what your client is thinking

- Your best chance to close

- A question

- Your moments to discover what

  your client believes in and what

  they fear

With objections, you'll discover the

primary reasons your client isn't

purchasing. When you answer their

question, you can empower them,

remove their fears, and close.

We must know what their objection is before we can close the sale. Ordinary people see resistance as a battle. Professional persuaders sit on the same side of the table with their clients. When people know you care about them, believe you are like them, and you come from an ethical perspective, you're able to build a long-term relationship with them. Professional influence and persuasion come from handling objections before they arise, by pre-framing them in advance.

For example: *"I realize the investment of our product/service is challenging, we have the investment, because our system/product consistently produces 6 figure opportunities. That's what sets us apart from the average!"*

Minimize, Reduce, and Eliminate Objections

- Compare the objection to a benefit you have that will overwhelm it
- Give to others, and they will give back to you
- Build massive amounts of rapport
- Test close often

- Pre-frame objections and take

care of them before they

become a big problem

How To Transform Client

Objections Into Client

Commitments

a.   **Ignore the objection the first**

time it comes up; it may have been

an unconscious reflex reaction. We

can avoid this by asking open-ended

questions that don't end in yes or no.

The Most Considerable Challenges That Average Salespeople Face Are:

- The belief that objections are a fight or a battle to be won
- Trying to go after everything they believe is an objection;

wasting time with fake customer

resistance

- Fear of clients objecting

b. **Listen if the same objection**

comes up a second time by hearing

them out and letting them do the

majority of the speaking. Let the

client vent, and they'll eventually

run out of energy, often solving their

objection.

c. **Repeat** the objection back in

the form of a question. Repeating

puts people in a position to clarify

their words.

For example, the client says: *"I don't have the money!" You say: "You don't have the money?" and then stop... and listen.*

d.   **Dig Deeper:** This is where you're going to find out if what they said is the real objection. *"I'm sure you have a reason for saying that, what is it?"* Listen carefully to their answer; this is a definite moment where you can close the sale.

e.   **Turn the Objection into Commitment:** Whatever their objection is, if you can solve that

objection, would the client be ready

to move forward. *"If we could show*

you how to free up your time, using

our services, the way that you said

you want to. In your opinion, do you

feel you'd want to get started?"

Exercise:

What are two of the most common objections you face regularly? Write them out and how you'll respond using the first five steps.

<u>Objection 1:</u>

Response:

<u>Objection 2:</u>

Response:

VI. Put the client at ease: By sitting on the same side of the table with the client, siding with them, being understanding, respectful, agreeable, and appreciative of their perspective. *"I often..."He also..."They to..."* also make sure that you're aligning with them by saying things like: *"I agree and..." "I appreciate this about you and..." "I respect **X** about you and..."*

VII. Objections Are Questions: The question is how can we solve

_____ (Repeat their question

back to them) and give you _____ (2-

3 Benefits) That's the real question.

Right?

VIII. Answer your Step 7 Question:

By asking another question back at

them and focusing on their pain

points.

For example: *"So then isn't the real*

question, how can we get you _____

(Whatever Benefit the client is most

interested in) and if we don't do this,

wouldn't it cost you _____

(Whatever pain points they've expressed)

- Be curious and think, *"Why would this client be bringing up this objection or asking me these questions after they already expressed why they need my products/services?"*

- Outweigh their objection with a question on value:

Example: *"Can't we agree you receiving **X...Y...Z...** is more important than this concern?"*

- Explain your way through the objection

Example: *"You'll have a team of people dedicated to your needs, which will save you those five days it was taking you to complete this work yourself."*

- Deny the objection tactfully

  Example: *"It doesn't cost too much when you look at our competition and compare the benefits you receive from us. Here are three of our largest competitors for you to see."*

- Reduce the objection by taking the investment and breaking it down by its daily cost. **For example, 100/year = $8.33/month = about $0.27/Day** *"Are you going to let your health continue to suffer over $0.27 a day when you expressed you would do anything to feel better?"*

- **Gain client agreement and test close:** *"By doing **X** that would solve that problem, wouldn't it?*

(If they say **yes**, then proceed
with a test closing question like
the one below)

- *In your opinion, how do you see
  yourself using **X** when you get
  started?"* (If they say **no,** move
  back to step 4 and dig deeper to
  find out their WHY)

Take an Assumptive Posture And Validate the Client

- Congratulate clients when they make a decision—follow-up with a closing question.
- *"Congratulations! Could you spell your first and last name for me, please?"*

Step 9 Final Assignment

Get together with a friend or family member and have them pretend they're the client objecting to you. Practice using these steps to guide the objections towards resolution and closing the sale.

["Your future is created by what you do today, not tomorrow."] -

Robert Kiyosaki –

Sales Step 10: Create A Lasting Relationship And Make Buying Simple

The home stretch! Great job! You've made it here through persistence, drive, taking action, and putting in the work necessary to get results. At this point, you're not like everyone else. You're one of the elite, with the tools of the elite. You now have almost everything you need to be a genuinely exceptional persuader. If you've been practicing, I know you feel stable and confident at this point. There is one last

step to add to your toolbelt, and this step, I

believe, is the MOST important of them all!

Here Is What You'll Learn:

- To create positive, lifetime

  friendships with your clients;

  friendships where you grow

  together.
- Setting up the next sale through

  referrals and creating a mutually

  profitable relationship.

- Help the client to avoid feeling any forms of remorse for their purchase

At this point, you're ready for the real closing, or as I like to see it, the "opening" of a new life long relationship.

Make Buying Simple

- Pre-frame objections and handle them before Step 10.

- Serve your clients and provide additional value like a gift they weren't expecting.

- Always stay aligned with your client, don't get defensive or go on the attack if they raise another objection in Step 10.

Closing Strategies

- Congratulate them on the decision they've made (assuming)

- Tell a joke and get them laughing before the close

- Validate their decision to purchase by assuring them it's the right time

For example: *"It's excellent that you're getting this now. Soon, this won't be accessible the way it is today, because of our high demand."*

- Open your application form and begin filling it out with them

- Give them different choices by asking a question

For example: *"Would you like this, big or small? Today or tomorrow? Red or white?"*

- Give your client some decision-making power with a smaller decision

For example: *"How would you like this order shipped?"*

Buyer's Remorse

Sometimes after a purchase, a client feels guilt or remorse for what they've done. The excitement wears off, and they're left wondering if they made the right decision. Sometimes, it's their friends or significant others that criticize them for making this decision. To prevent this, we must create a long-term relationship between the client and the product/service. We have to create a future, so they understand what they'll be doing with their purchase down the road. Right after you persuade them professionally and make the sale, engage the clients' imagination by asking a question about their future with your product/service. Have them describe to you how their future looks with your product/service and how it will benefit them in years ahead.

For example: *"What will you be doing in **X** years, now that you have this? How do you see yourself?"*

Since your client has seen the future, with their purchase, they have justified what they've purchased. If anyone criticizes their decision, they can tell them what they'll be doing with it in the future. *"I got this health drink because It's going to be the perfect drink to use for the next year while I lose weight"* or *"I invested in their services, because two years from now, the time we saved will triple our returns."*

Gaining Referrals

At this point, you've built a strong relationship with your client. It's time to leverage your effort and ask for referrals. There is a right way and a wrong way to ask for them.

Asking For A Referral

"My business can only grow through people who trust me and tell other people about the service I provided them. Those people refer me to people who can benefit the most from my services. How has my service been to you? If I offered you exceptional service, would you do me a favor? Who are five people you know that could also benefit from my services?"

- Encourage your clients to support you and ask them to personally call a couple of their referrals to provide positive feedback on you.
- Provide your client incentives, like gifts or compensation for successful referrals.

- Expect and believe you will receive referrals.

- Be prepared by finding out as much information as possible about your references before you speak with them.

- It's great to ask for referrals, whether you make the sale or not. A reference can save you a lot of calls.

How To Contact Referrals

- **Keep a Referral File:** Keep referrals in alphabetical order, with 13 sections. Contact A's and B's in the first week, C's and D's in week two, and so on. You'll reach two letters of the alphabet each week, which will make contact with each of your clients at minimum four times a year.

- **Third-Party Compliments:** Using these compliments is a great way to get referrals attention immediately. Most people engage a reference by saying: "*Hi, my name is X from Y* *company, and your friend **Z** told*

me I should give you a call

because you might like this."

Don't fall into this trap. You won't

get the clients' attention because

they don't care about your name or

your company.

A Better Way

*"Hi **X,** you don't know me; however,*

*we have a mutual friend whose name is **Y**.*

He/she shared something with me, about

you, that I thought was incredible (share the

previous compliment), and he/she thought

you would benefit from what we have here.

*By the way, my name is **A** from **B** company.*

Step 10 Final Assignment

Consider a client, from the past that you haven't closed a sale with yet. A vital client that feels like they "got away" Go back through your notes here, to solidify what you learned, and prepare yourself. Make a promise to yourself that you will arm yourself with this knowledge and make that contact again within 30 days.

Fear has two meanings: Forget Everything and Run or Face

Everything and Rise. The choice is

yours."] - Zig Ziglar –

Final Thoughts

Congratulations on reaching this
point! By completing this book, you created
a unique framework that will help you
empower others to say *yes* to you and your
offerings. Whatever goods or services you
provide, they're valuable and more people
need your help. My sincere wish for you is
that you use this information to serve
people and help them make that one
decision that will change their life. While
these are ten steps that flow cohesively,
focus on improving one step at a time;

instead of memorizing all ten stages and trying to execute them rigidly. No matter which action you focus on, it will enhance the other steps. For example, imagine that you only concentrate on level 1 (Preparation). If all you did was focus on being more prepared before initiating contact with clients. Can you see how this would improve the steps that followed? Communication with clients would be more meaningful, and you'd reach your peak emotional state quickly because you felt more prepared. How about if you only focused on following-up with your clients? Can you see how this would improve everything else, including your return

clients?

Focus on one skill at a time, master

it, and move to the next until you've

learned all ten steps. At that point, this

process will be as effortless as breathing.

Also, the growth you'll have undergone to

get to that level of mastery will transform

yours and your families' quality of life. It will

enable you to contribute more than you

ever thought!

Would you do me a favor? Would

you leave a review for this book? It would

be a tremendous help for others who want

to take their life to level 10. I appreciate

you, I'm grateful for your time, and I look

forward to hearing your success story.

Below I've also included the first chapter of

my book; *You Are Successful*. I believe you'll

take some great insights away and learn

habits you can use to crank your success to

the next level! With gratitude, Wes Lee

Bonus Chapter from *You Are Successful*

by Wes Lee

CHAPTER ONE

What is a habit?

Habits are the small decisions and actions you take every day. Your habits account for about 40 percent of your behavior, and your life's the sum of them.

Everyone has habits, good or bad! You began developing habits from a young age, such as sucking a thumb, napping every afternoon, or leaving the lights on. These behaviors are part of our routines.

Do you see the power of a habit? Take a moment and list some of your most essential practices. What patterns would you like to keep? Which ones do you want to remove? We know that not all habits are good for us. Many of us recognize the need to get rid of bad habits or cultivate new habits that empower us. And that's why we seek guidance through self-help books, the internet, advice from friends, family, and consultants. A "habit" in psychology, is any regularly repeated behavior that requires little or no thought; it's learned rather than innate. A pattern can be part of any activity, from eating and sleeping to thinking and reacting. Patterns will develop through reinforcement and repetition. *Reinforcing* encourages the *repetition* of a behavior or response. Every time the stimulus is triggered, the action occurs. The practice becomes more automatic with each repetition. However, some habits can be formed based on a single experience, usually when emotions are involved.

How do habits influence

our success?

Your habits show your unique identity to the world. However, sometimes people forget that their habits also affect their success. It's essential to know how your patterns change how you succeed. Your practices reflect who you are and form your unique identity. For example, some people get up early, while others sleep-in. Your sleep patterns a habit that starts your day. And we get so used to the daily routines that we don't realize they're influencing our lives. If someone wants to be successful, they need to think about everything they do or don't do. Each of their practices shows their commitment. Being successful depends mostly on the habits you engage in repeatedly, which ultimately shapes your life. Your habits will make or break your existence, as they directly influence your happiness. Some patterns are more powerful than others; your daily habits determine your attitude and future progress. So, before you decide to design your success patterns, define how your current practices are helping or hurting you.

Bad habits are a distraction:

Most people have various kinds of bad habits, like spending too much, lying, or even gossiping. These habits affect productivity and lower the chances of success. To achieve what you want, we need to kill the bad habits that are hurting your progress.

Habits are the result of your decisions:

Whichever patterns you choose to adopt, it's your decision. So, when you select an excellent habit, think about how it's right for your goals; your habits determine your destiny. If you choose to read inspirational biographies, do it because

you linked biographies to your vision.

Time-management reflects in your habits:

Whatever your patterns are, they need *time* before they can work. For instance, if you have a habit of watching television for hours, you're trading your time for that habit. Therefore, your good or bad habits affect your time and your long-term success. Think of time as the most valuable currency we can never get back; we're always spending it. Where are you spending yours?

Developing good habits is in your control:

It is crucial to remember that only you control the development of your habits.

When you adopt patterns that serve you, you'll increase your chances of success. But, you're the only one that can focus your attention on those patterns. Also, wherever your attention goes, you'll get more of that.

How to build new habits for success

Some habits manifest in your daily life, often as things to do, from brushing your teeth to work; your life's the sum of your habits. The great news is, whatever success you define, the strategies are the same. Your *choices* impact your progress daily. Develop different successful habits with these techniques, and you'll achieve your set goals. Set *clear* and *specific* goals that are important to you. If your goals don't inspire and scare you, you won't reach them; make sure you feel passion for them. Focus on no more than *two* goals, quality over quantity. Having a list of goals is only useful with a tight focus; don't spread yourself thin, and don't multi-task. Describe your goals in detail, so you develop your vision. Vague goals equal vague results. After identifying your *two* goals, add why they're essential to achieve. Many people get bogged down and stop at the start, so get emotional and take advantage of the drive you feel to take action. Now, you're ready to learn practical strategies for developing habits, improving your health, productivity, and achieving your goals.

Identify the empowering habit you want to adopt:

First, you need to choose your patterns. Trying to develop ten new habits at the same time will waste your time. Focus on a practice you want to build, and you can always add multiple patterns in the following months, preferably after mastering your first habit. For now, identify a habit you want to develop and write it down. Practices might include: getting up at 5 a.m., for the gym four days a week, reading a book for 30 minutes a day, or journaling at least 1000 words every day. Whatever habits you choose, ensure that you commit to doing them every day; consistency is critical.

Make a decision:

Decide to act a specific way 100 percent of the time; your habits are your lifestyle. Let's say you choose to get up early and train every morning. Wear your workout clothes to sleep, set your clock to a

specific time, and when the alarm sounds,

get up right away, and start training. You're

not just training to train; you're doing it

because you identify as a healthy person.

Choose the discipline over your mood:

Imagine if you only trained on the

days when you felt fabulous. If your

workouts depend on whether you feel

blissful, they probably won't be consistent.

Decide what actions you plan to take,

regardless of your mood. Taking action

when you don't feel like it, trains your

discipline. You'll be proud to keep your

schedule, and this mindset works for any goal. Remember, you can pay the price tomorrow, or you can pay the price today, sooner or later we all pay the price. Your *tomorrow* won't be more comfortable until you decide to *do* today. When you feel like quitting (and we all do), remember your *why* for starting this journey. Remember who you'll be years from now when you breakthrough. This year's going to go by anyway, make it your record year.

Focus on the big picture:

One of the main steps in developing lifelong habits is to envision them in your future. In other words, what are your long-term goals? For example, if you want to create a new pattern to write every day, see yourself as a best-selling author. An effective way to focus on the big picture is, to begin with, the end in mind; envision your end goal every day. Studies show that abstract thinking helps you develop the self-discipline to build and maintain new habits. However, there's a caveat. You need to avoid daydreaming and create visualization exercises. Create an *actionable* plan and link it to your internal motivation (your "why"). Your inner motivation is your desire for an intrinsic (rather than an external) reward. A powerful question to ask is, "why do I want to build this new habit?" Think about the reason behind your desire. Once you identify your "why," how can you create more "internal" motivation? When you create your action plan around your "why," you're supporting your new habit.

I used to work with a high-paying real estate company, and one of the first exercises we did was to draw out our "why." The position was commissioned-based, and the average starting income was $150,000 per year. However, the average work hours per week were 80. So, our "why" was critical. This story's remarkable because the people that thrived were always motivated by the things you can't purchase, while the quitters focused on stuff. You knew someone was going to be successful when they concentrated on needs such as love, gratitude, and contribution. However, the unsuccessful always wanted better cars, bigger houses, and more stuff. What feeling are you looking get from your new habit, and what small action will you take to get closer to that feeling? There's no right or wrong answer, just the action that works for you.

Incorporate the habit with a program:

After identifying your pattern, create a schedule. This step is crucial because the success of your new practice depends on your commitment to consistency. It's your schedule that will force you to develop the new habit, your tool for accountability. If the pattern you want to establish is reading for 30 minutes per day, what time will you read every day? Similarly, if you're going to exercise in the gym every day, what time do you want it to happen, and for how long? For example, you choose to hit the gym at 6 a.m. and train for an hour. You're setting aside *time* for this objective, and you're dedicating yourself to training every day.

Whether you want to train, or don't, you

just do it because you commit to yourself.

Never allow an exception:

Don't create exceptions to your new

pattern. There are no excuses or

rationalizations. We need to be able to keep

promises to ourselves before anyone else. If

you decide to get up at 6 a.m. every day, get

up at 6 a.m. every day! You need conscious

consistency until it becomes automatic.

Create a model of consistency. No one has

to remind you to breathe, right? It's

automatic. What other patterns can you

automate? Maybe it's cardio exercises on

Monday, Wednesday, and Friday and strength training on Tuesday and Thursday. Or, take an hour every morning and practice a new social media strategy to promote your business. Find habits that support your goals, and then automate them so you can make steady (daily) progress. Persistence replaces talent, genetics, and luck. There can be no real success without it.

Get Back Up:

We have a natural tendency to give up a new habit, especially after we fail to take action or make a mistake. In the early stages of creating a new pattern, your mind will find every possible excuse to leave the ship and return to your old ways. It's even more difficult when your environment doesn't support the change. The more aware you are of the tricks your mind plays, the faster you'll crush them and master your new habit. Be aware that the tendency to stop will occur. Execute the pattern anyway, even if you feel like you're going *through the motions.*

What is your reward?

At first, people do something because there's a reward, and a habit develops through that cycle. What's the incentive you receive after training in the gym? How would you reward yourself after spending your time reading for 30 minutes a day? If you want to develop a habit, you need the reward. For example, after journaling 1,000-words, grab a snack, rest for a few minutes, or allow yourself to check Instagram. Create something, so your mind knows there's a definite incentive to do the work. Rewards compel people to get into the habit of acting. So, for your daily habits, create little rewards for yourself. After a while, you can replace several smaller prizes with a larger one. For instance, taking a night out to get drinks with friends, monthly trips to the movies, or spa. Spoil yourself; make yourself feel luxurious for your accomplishments.

Create declarations:

Create statements that you can declare to the world, over and over again. Repeating declarations out loud increases the speed that you'll develop your new habits. For example, you might say, "I'm a champion, I'm changing this world, and I focus on giving" Repeat your declarations before falling asleep. You'll notice that you'll start to become anything you say you are. For added results, say your created statements to yourself in the mirror.

Track your progress:

When setting your goals, you have a few benchmarks to assess how you're doing. It's easy to get excited about a new target at first. Still, the results depend on the consistency of your actions every day. At the start of a new month, check-in with yourself. Is your plan working? What isn't working? Determine what's working and do more of that, determine what doesn't work, pivot, and drop that action. If an activity doesn't work, it doesn't work. Don't work harder to try to fit a square peg in a round hole. When you regularly track your progress, there's a bonus; you stay connected to your goals. However, you need to be open-minded and fluid, be ready to kill anything that doesn't serve you. The reason why people give up so fast is that they tend to look at how far they still have to go, instead of recognizing the progress they've already made.

Create success by developing good habits:

So where do you go from here? Limit your focus to developing one empowering habit every 30 days. The more you try to do, the less you'll achieve. More isn't always more beautiful. It's better to be *all-in* on one project than *half-committed* to ten. Successful people master their actions because they excel at the fundamentals. They focus and exercise the basics every day. Ordinary people, on the other hand, don't see the importance of fundamentals. They look for the next big idea or new trend (shiny objects). That's why people achieve their goals when they practice consistency and discipline. Setting goals isn't something you do once; your goals are living; they need your attention every day. If you want results, start here. Master the fundamentals by developing exceptional habits.

Check out *You Are Successful* on Amazon here: https://tinyurl.com/yaoc72qf

Next Steps

Also by Wes Lee

Impactful Leadership

You Have A Purpose

You Are Rich

You Are Free

You Are Successful

The Brave Bunch (Children's Book)

Read more at amazon.com/author/wes_lee

About the Author

Wes Lee is a passionate advocate for success with over a decade of experience and a business degree from Hawaii Pacific University. Best known for his Leadership in the Army and operating multiple successful businesses, including lending money in 42 states, starting a business that significantly reduces health-care costs, and taking ownership in a life insurance company. Lee's books take his hard-won experience and translate it into easy recipes you can follow to achieve massive breakthroughs. His site https://twitter.com/wes_lee_success shares strategies and resources to have everything you want from life while getting paid handsomely. Wes loves living in Kapolei, Hawaii (a personal dream) with his wife and digging his toes in the sand at the lagoons of Ko'olina.

Follow at
https://www.tiktok.com/@weslee1988